Phonics Touch & Trace

Written by Lisa Holt

Illustrator Peter Reddy

Based on characters originated by Lyn Wendon

About Letterland

Letterland is an imaginary place where letters come to life! The friendly Letterland characters help children to easily understand the sound and shape of letters – one of the key skills needed when learning to read and write.

Simple stories about the Letterland characters explain letter sounds and shapes, so that confusion over similar looking letters is avoided and children are motivated to listen, think and learn.

One of Letterland's keys to success is its 'sound trick'. By just starting to pronounce a character's name, such as '**a**...' (Annie Apple), '**b**...' (Bouncy Ben), '**c**...' (Clever Cat), a child automatically says the correct letter sound. It's that simple! The combination of memorable characters and proven educational principles makes Letterland the ideal way to introduce your child to the alphabet.

For more information, including a pronunciation guide for all the letter sounds, see: **www.letterland.com**

| Annie Apple | Bouncy Ben | Clever Cat | Dippy Duck | Eddy Elephant | Firefighter Fred | Golden Girl |

| Noisy Nick | Oscar Orange | Peter Puppy | Quarrelsome Queen | Red Robot | Sammy Snake | Talking Tess |

About this book

The *Phonics Touch & Trace* book is designed for you to share with your child. They will think of it all as simply fun, but with your help, they'll be learning all about letter shapes, sounds and building an awareness of words.

Letter shapes - Children can finger-trace the textured letter shapes on each page. The dots and arrows help with starting positions and correct letter formation. (Where there are two arrows, the first stroke is shown by the longest arrow). The handwriting verses in the corners of each page further reinforce correct letter formation in a language children can easily relate to.

Letter sounds - Have fun emphasising the sound again and again as you read the stories aloud then look for all the objects that start with the same sound as the featured Letterlander. You can check list at the back of the book to see how many you have spotted. Play with letter sounds. Decide what the Letterlanders would like to eat, drink or do. For example, Bouncy Ben might like to eat bread and butter, Clever Cat may like a cup of cocoa. Would Firefighter Fred prefer a cup of tea or a fresh fruit drink?

Explore - Have fun talking about where the objects are and let your child decide what might happen next. For example, do you think the helicopter will land on the hillside so the pilot can buy a hat from Harry Hat Man's shop? On a second or third read, you could ask your child to tell you all about each picture. Listen carefully as your child points out all the objects that start with the featured sound, and tells you what is going on in each picture.

Harry Hat Man   Impy Ink   Jumping Jim   Kicking King   Lucy Lamp Light   Munching Mike

Uppy Umbrella   Vicky Violet   Walter Walrus   Fix-it Max   Yellow Yo-yo Man   Zig Zag Zebra

In an apple orchard in Letterland there is a little talking apple called **Annie Apple**.

She loves to swing in the trees like an acrobat and chat to her animal friends. Can you spot any of her friends in the picture?

She is a very happy little apple who is often very active, appearing in lots of words. You can hear her saying '**a**' in words like:

ant   **apple**   **arrow**

Handwriting Verse

Brush down Ben's big, long ears. Go up and round his head so his face appears!

Bouncing around Letterland there is a little bunny rabbit called **Bouncy Ben**.

Bouncy Ben has six brothers and he lives in a burrow in a riverbank by a big bridge.

Bouncy Ben is often very busy bouncing around making his little '**b**' sound in words like:

ball   boat   book

Handwriting Verse
Curve round Clever Cat's face to begin. Then gently tickle her under her chin. ♫

Let's say, 'Hello,' to the Letterland cat. She lives in a little cottage near the Letterland castle and she's called **Clever Cat**. Why? Because she can do so many clever things. She can even count! Can you count, too?

There's another thing you should know about Clever Cat. She doesn't 'miaow'. That's because she is a Letterland cat. She makes a little '**c**' sound instead. You can hear it at the start of words like:

cake   car   cup

Down by the duckpond in Letterland you'll meet a delightful duck called **Dippy Duck**. She loves dipping her head under the water and diving down deep to find duckweed to eat for her dinner.

Do you know she doesn't quack like other ducks? She makes a little '**d**' sound as she waddles into words like:

dad   **dog**   **drum**

Handwriting Verse
Ed has a headband.
Draw it and then
stroke round his head
and his trunk to the end.

Here's **Eddy Elephant**. He's enjoying eating a boiled egg for his mid-morning snack at eleven o'clock. He thinks eggs are the best! They give him lots of energy when he is exercising, or doing his Elephant-on-End trick!

Eddy Elephant says '**e**' in words like:

 **egg**   **elbow**   **envelope**

Handwriting Verse
First draw Fred's helmet.
Then go down a way.
Give him some arms
and he'll put out the blaze.

Here comes **Firefighter Fred**. He's a friendly firefighter who looks after everyone in Letterland. Fred is fit and fearless. If ever a fire gets out of control, he rushes off in his fire engine with his friend, Frank, and they put out the flames with lots of foam.

His sound is a bit like foam coming from a hose. Put your teeth on your lips and gently blow, '**fff**'. Then say:

fish fire frog

Handwriting Verse 🎵
Go round Golden Girl's head.
Go down her golden hair.
Then curve to make her swing,
so she can sit there.

It's a glorious day in the Letterland garden and **Golden Girl** is enjoying swinging on her garden swing and watching all her lovely plants grow.

She has just gulped down some grape juice. Can you see the empty glass? Did you hear her making her '**g**...**g**...' sound as she gulped? She's not greedy. She just thinks it's funny to make a gulping sound when she drinks. You'll also hear her making that sound in words like:

garden **gate** **grass**

Handwriting Verse
Hurry from the Hat Man's head down to his heel on the ground. Go up and bend his knee over, so he'll hop while he makes his sound.

Harry Hat Man lives in a house halfway up a hill. He makes hundreds of hats to sell in his hat shop. Let's say, 'Hello', to Harry Hat Man.

Hold on! I forgot to tell you... he hates noise. That's why, when he goes into words, he only whispers his sound. Look! He doesn't even wear shoes because he thinks they make too much noise as he hops along. So let's just whisper, 'Hello', to Harry. 'Hello!' You can hear him whispering '**hhh**' in words like:

hand   **hat**   **house**

Handwriting Verse
Inside the ink bottle
draw a line.
Add an inky dot.
That's fine!

In Letterland there is an incredible little ink bottle called **Impy Ink**. He's incredible because his ink bottle has the seven colours of the rainbow inside it. He has even invented a way to write in rainbow-coloured ink.

You will see Impy Ink's thin little letter with a dot on top in lots and lots of words. He says '**i**' in words like:

in   insect   ink

High above Letterland you may see **Jumping Jim**. There are just two things that Jumping Jim really enjoys: Jumping and juggling. Look at him jumping and juggling at the same time! You can only ever see one ball as the others are moving so fast.

As he jumps into words he says, '**j**'. Listen:

jam   jet   juice

Handwriting Verse
Kicking King's body
is a straight stick.
Add his arm, then his leg,
so he can kick.

Kicking King lives with Quarrelsome Queen in the Letterland castle. He's one of the kindest men you will ever meet. He has to be to keep the peace, living with such a quarrelsome queen!

Kicking King likes nothing better than kicking a football about. That's why he's called the kicking king. When he goes into words he makes a '**k**' sound. You can hear it in words like:

kettle　　　**key**　　　**kitchen**

Living in the Letterland Lighthouse is a lovely lady called **Lucy Lamp Light**. When she smiles everything lights up around her. She helps anyone who is lost or lonely by lighting the way for them.

The lovely sound she makes is '**lll**'. Listen for it in words like:

leg   log   lion

15

Handwriting Verse ♩
Make Munching Mike's back leg first, then his second leg, and third, so he can go munch-munching in a word.

Let's meet **Munching Mike**! Munching Mike is a metal monster. But he's not a scary monster. He's the mildest monster you'll ever meet. He likes to munch on a mixture of things like mangoes, marshmallows and mushrooms. He also munches bits of metal and magnets!

Can you hear him saying '**mmm**' as he munches? He says '**mmm**' in words like:

man   **map**   **milk**

Handwriting Verse
'Now bang my nail,'
Noisy Nick said.
'Go up and over
around my head.'

In Letterland there is a boy called **Noisy Nick**. Nick is nine years old. He is called Noisy Nick because he loves making noise. He likes hammering nails and banging on his drum. His next door neighbours are not so keen on all the noise he makes!

Nick says '**nnn**' in words like:

nine   **noodles**   **nose**

In Letterland you will often meet a little talking orange called **Oscar Orange**. Oscar works in an office at the Letterland docks. Often there are lots of odd objects at the docks. Lots of boxes, too. Oscar loves to sit on top of the boxes to watch what's going on.

You can hear Oscar saying '**o**' in words like:

on   off   orange

Handwriting Verse
♪ Pat Peter Puppy properly.
First stroke down his ear,
then up and round his face
so he won't shed a tear.

This is **Peter Puppy**. He's a perfect pal for everyone. He's very playful and he has pleasing, floppy ears that droop down – perfect for patting.

Pretend to give him a little pat now.

Peter Puppy says '**p**' in words like:

paint　　　　**pen**　　　　**pencil**

Handwriting Verse
Quickly go round the Queen's cross face. Then comb her beautiful hair into place.

Did you know there is a **Quarrelsome Queen** in Letterland who never goes anywhere without her royal umbrella? She quarrels with everyone. That's why, when you see her in a word, she has her back to the other letters. She doesn't mean to quarrel all the time. In fact, sometimes she goes and sits in her quiet room just to calm herself down.

You can hear her quietly saying her '**qu**' sound in words like:

quarter   question   quilt

This little rascal is called **Red Robot**. He's a rascal because he is always running off with things that don't belong to him and that's not right!

He gets very excited when he sees things that begin with his sound. He rolls his tongue and growls, '**rrr**'. You can hear him growling '**rrr**' in words like:

rain   rice   river

Handwriting Verse
Start at Sam's head
where he can see.
Stroke down to his tail,
oh so care-ful-ly!

This is **Sammy Snake**. He loves the seaside. Sometimes he speeds about on the sea, but most of all he likes to sunbathe on the sand. He always takes care of his skin in the sun and slaps on lots of sun cream. Sometimes, Sammy wears a sun hat and sunglasses, too.

Sammy Snake hisses his sound, like this, '**sss**'. You can hear him hissing at the start of words like:

sand   **sea**   **sun**

Handwriting Verse

Tall as a tower make Talking Tess stand. Go from head to toe, and then from hand to hand.

It's time to meet the tallest lady in Letterland. She's called **Talking Tess** and she's always talking. She talks on the telephone all day long. She even takes her tiny telephone on trains and in taxis as she travels about. She works in Teletouch Tower and it is her job to keep everyone in Letterland in touch with each other.

Talking Tess says '**t**' in words like:

ten   train   tree

Handwriting Verse
Under the umbrella
draw a shape like a cup.
Then draw a straight line
so it won't tip up.

Do you have an umbrella? When it rains you can get under an umbrella so you don't get wet. There are two little children under an umbrella in this picture. Can you see them?

The cheerful umbrella floating up in the sky in Letterland is called **Uppy Umbrella**. Let's pretend to put up an umbrella and make her sound, '**u**'. She says '**u**' in words like:

 up   **umbrella**   **under**

Handwriting Verse
Very neatly,
start at the top.
Draw down your vase,
then up and stop.

Here is **Vicky Violet** digging up the vegetables she has grown in the valley near her village. The soil is very rich near the volcano and her vegetables are full of vitamins. She takes very good care of her plants. She especially loves the violets that she keeps in a valuable vase.

Vicky's violets are very special because they can talk! They make the '**vvv**' sound at the start of her name. You can hear them saying '**vvv**' in words like:

 van

vegetables

 vet

Handwriting Verse 🎵
When you draw the Walrus wells,
with wild and wavy water,
whizz down and up and then,
whizz down and up again.

Are you wondering who you can see in this window? Well, this is **Walter Walrus**. Walter loves water. You'll often see him wallowing by the Letterland waterfall. He likes to rest in the sunshine and wedge his webbed flippers into the water wells of his letter shape.

The weather looks quite windy in Letterland today. When the wind blows it sounds a bit like Walter Walrus's sound, '**www**'. You can hear him saying '**w**' in words like:

water   watch   window

This little boy is called **Fix-it Max**. He's just six years old. He's called Fix-it Max because he is so good at fixing things. Often, when he has fixed something he gives it back with a note saying:

All fixed! Love from Max xxx

His sound is like a little kiss. You can hear him whisper **'k-ss'** in words like:

box   fox   six

Handwriting Verse ♫
You first make the yo-yo sack
on the Yo-yo Man's back,
and then go down to his toes
so he can sell his yo-yos.

This is **Yellow Yo-yo Man**. He's called Yellow Yo-yo Man because he wears yellow clothes and he sells yo-yos. He's been selling yo-yos for years. He's trying to save up to buy a yacht.

If you were in Letterland you might hear him yelling, 'Yo-yos... yellow yo-yos for sale!'

His sound is '**y**'. It is at the start of words like:

yellow   yogurt   yo-yo

Letterland Zoo

In Letterland you may be lucky enough to see **Zig Zag Zebra**. She is very shy and she zooms about the Letterland Zoo. She's such a fast runner she has even won prizes.

Because she is shy, you don't see her in many words. Listen to her little '**zzz**' sound in words like:

zero   zip   zoo

The *Phonics Touch & Trace* book is designed for you to share with your children. They will think of it all as simply fun, but with your help, they'll be learning important first reading, speaking and listening skills. To start with, look for all the objects that start with the same sound as the featured Letterlander. The **a-z** list below includes most, but not all of them! Play with letter sounds. Decide what the Letterlanders would like to eat, drink, do. Accept all answers, but give special praise for answers beginning with the Letterlander's sound, for example, bread and butter for Bouncy Ben, carrot cake for Clever Cat. Would Firefighter Fred prefer a cup of cocoa or a fresh fruit drink?

Have fun talking about where the objects are and let your child decide what might happen next. For example, do you think the helicopter will land on the hillside so the pilot can buy a hat from Harry Hat Man's shop? On a second or third read, you could ask your child to tell you all about each picture. Listen carefully as your child points out all the objects that start with the featured sounds, and tells you what is going on in each picture.

Things to find

a	d	grass	k	o	rice	u	y
alligator	dad	green	kettle	octopus	river	umbrellas	yak
ant	daffodils		key	off	rocket	under	yacht
antelope	dog	**h**	king	olives	rocks	up	yawn
apple	dragonfly	hand	kitchen	on	roses	upside down	yellow
apple tree	drum	hat	kittens	orange	rubbish		yo-yo
arrow	duck	head		ostrich	rucksack	**v**	yogurt
	duck pond	hedge	**l**		ruler	van	
b		heel	lamb	**p**		vegetables	**z**
bag	**e**	helicopter	leg	paper	**s**	vet	zip
ball	eggs	hen	lemons	paint	sailboat	village	zoo
baseball	elbow	hill	lighthouse	painting	sand	violets	zoom
bat	eleven o'clock	hive	lion	paw print	sandcastle	violin	
bee	envelope	horse	log	pen	sea	volcano	
bird		house	lolly	pencil	seaside		
bluebells	**f**			penguin	seaweed	**w**	
boat	fir trees	**i**	**m**	pink	smile	wall	
book	fire	iguana	man	puppy	speedboat	washing	
bridge	fish	in	map	purple	starfish	watch	
brother	fire engine	Indian flag	melon		stones	water	
bush	flowers	ink	milk	**q**	sun	waterfall	
	fox	ink pen	moth	quail		well	
c	frog	insect	mountain	question	**t**	wind	
cake	frying pan	inside	mushroom	quilt	ticket	window	
car				quince	trumpet	worm	
carrots	**g**	**j**	**n**	squirrel	toys		
castle	garden	jam	nail		train	**x**	
cat	gate	jar	newspaper	**r**	tiger	box	
clouds	geese	jeep	night	rabbits	trunk	fox	
cottage	girl	jelly	noodles	raccoon	tennis racket	hexagon	
cow	glass	jet	nose	radio	tree	six	
crow	goat	jigsaw	nuts	rain	teddy bear		
cup	grapes	juice		rainbow	telephone		
		jug		reeds			

Letterland

Child-friendly phonics

The Letterland system teaches all 44 sounds in the English language through stories rather than rules. There are resources to take children from the very first stages of learning to full literacy.

ABC Trilogy

Sticker & Activity Books

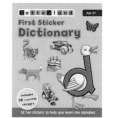

Picture Books

Games & Puzzles

See our full range at: **www.letterland.com**

For product advice and support: **info@letterland.com**

Published by Letterland International Ltd, Leatherhead, Surrey, KT22 9AD, UK.
© Letterland International 2013
Reprinted 2018.
10 9 8 7 6 5 4 3 2
ISBN: 978-1-86209-976-0
Product Code: TE95
LETTERLAND® is a registered trademark of Lyn Wendon.
Printed in China

Author: Lisa Holt
Illustrator: Peter Reddy
Designer: Beth Maddox
Editor & Originator of Letterland: Lyn Wendon